LOVE TO BE ME!

by Sarah Kraftchuk

Illustrated by Sari Richter

Second printing, 2015

Story and Creative Design by: Sarah Kraftchuk
Illustrations by: Sari Richter

Love To Be Me! may be ordered through booksellers or by contacting:

Love To Be Publications
Toronto, Ontario
www.lovetobeme.ca
416.319.3331

ISBN 978-0-9918941-0-9

Library and Archives Canada Cataloguing in Publication

Kraftchuk, Sarah, 1987-, author

　Love to be me! / Sarah Kraftchuk, Sari Richter.

ISBN 978-0-9918941-0-9 (bound)

1. Human body--Juvenile literature. 2. Body image--Juvenile literature. I. Richter, Sari, illustrator II. Title.

HM636.K73 2013   j306.4'613   C2013-902387-9

Printed in Canada.

This book is dedicated to you!

You deserve to be comfortable in your own skin, within your own world.

You deserve to be kindly recognized for exactly who you are.

Making the world a kinder place starts with being kind to yourself.

Express your love for who you are in this moment.

Dance freely within yourself.

Always remember,

You are enough!

♡ Sarah

I love my hands.

count

read

hold

greet

I can touch, feel and create.

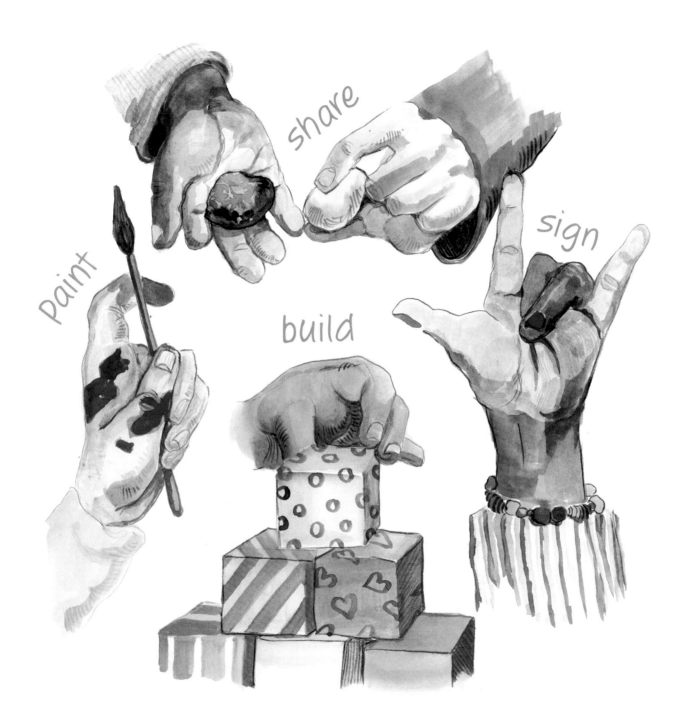

paint

share

sign

build

I love my tummy.

I can laugh,
digest my food and
nourish my body.

I love
my head.

I can think for myself,

imagine and wonder.

I love my mouth.

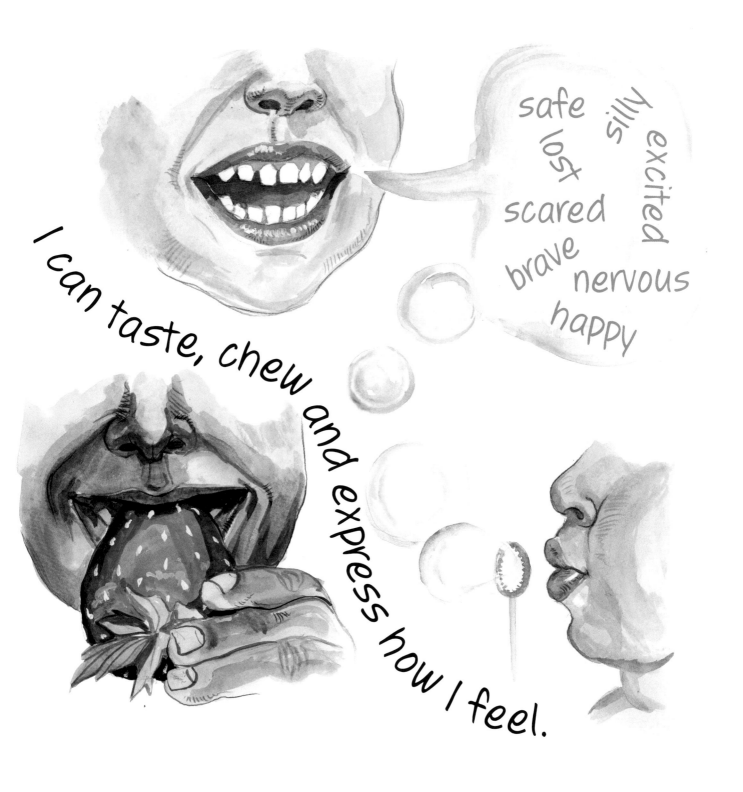

I can taste, chew and express how I feel.

safe
silly
lost
excited
scared
brave
nervous
happy

I love my nose.

I can breathe in the many scents of nature.

I discover
the environment
that
I'm a part of.

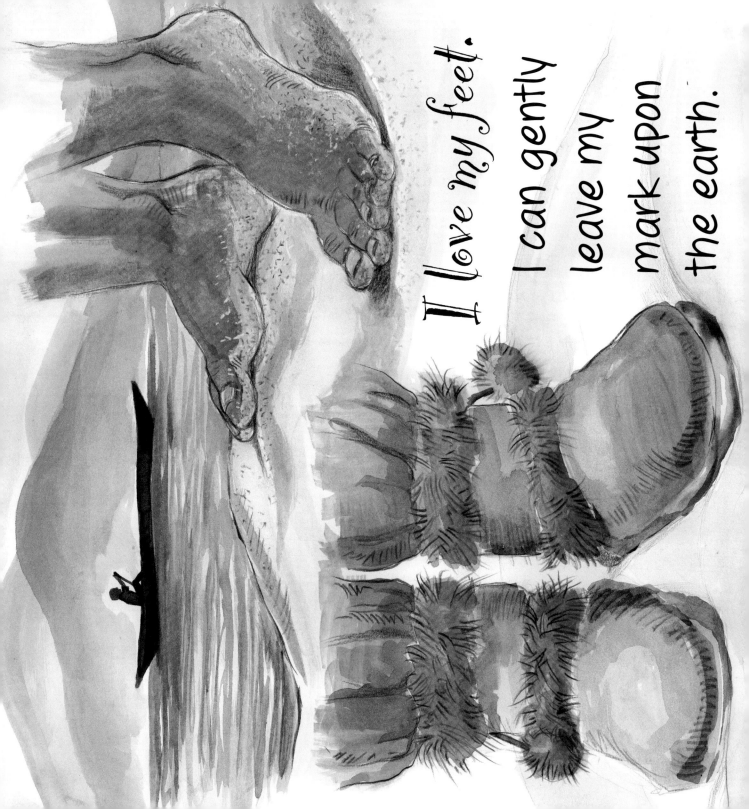

I love my feet.
I can gently
leave my
mark upon
the earth.

I love my arms.

I can reach out
and embrace
the world.

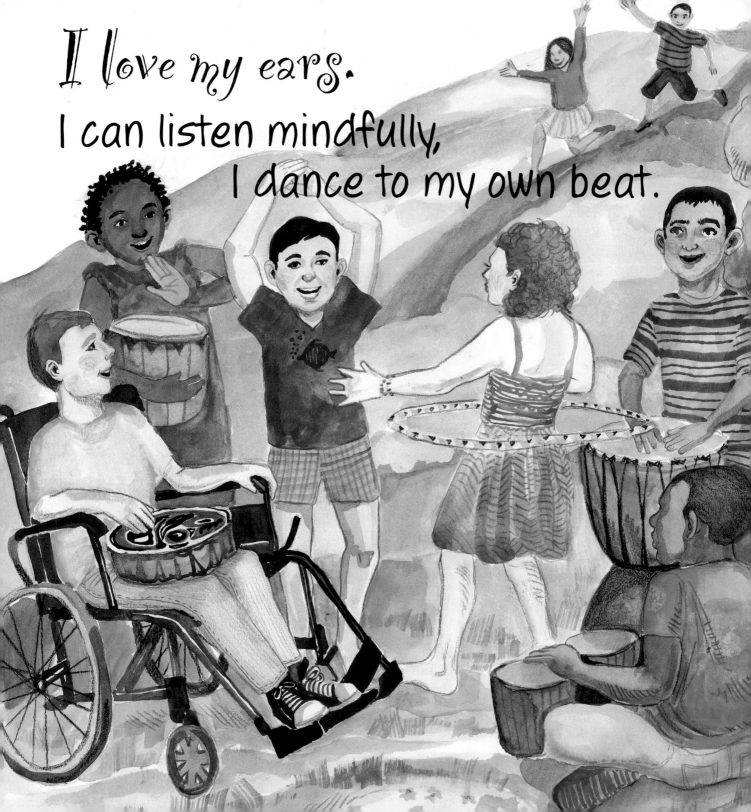

I love my ears.
I can listen mindfully,
I dance to my own beat.

I love my eyes.

I can see the beauty
in the world and in me.

I love my legs.

I love my chest.

It protects my heart.

I can give and receive love.

It protects my lungs.

I can breathe in and out.

I love
my body for all
it can do.

I
AM
grateful
TO BE ME!

"It's not what you look at that matters,
it's what you see."

Henry David Thoreau

Sarah Kraftchuk enjoys exploring the connection between body, mind and heart in a playful and interactive way. Sarah is a teacher, holistic nutritionist and mindfulness practitioner. Through poetry and illustrations, Sarah creates a space for self-exploration, inclusivity and open dialogue. Children and parents alike are encouraged to honour their inner sparkle and dance freely within themselves. **Spread l♥ve.**

Sari Richter (BFA, DTATI) grew up in Ancaster, Ontario and moved to Toronto to attend the Ontario College of Art and Design and subsequently the Toronto Art Therapy Institute. She is a certified art therapist and a practicing artist and illustrator. She explores acrylic paint, mixed media, digital video, embroidery, printmaking, collage, jewellery and animation.

I AM. Magical ME!
Story by Sarah Kraftchuk   Illustrated by Sari Richter

I AM. Magical ME! celebrates the magic that is inside each and every one of us. Connect mindfully and authentically to your feelings, thoughts, and emotions, and explore who you are, in this moment. **I AM. Magical ME!** invites readers to enjoy this journey of self-discovery, and to always remember that the magic is inside you! **www.lovetobeme.ca**